MENSA® for kds
EVERYDAY SUPER-SMART
MIND GAMES

100 Awesome Brain Teasers!

Sky Pony Press
New York

Sky Pony Press books may be purchased in bulk at special discounts for sales promotion, corporate gifts, fund-raising, or educational purposes. Special editions can also be created to specifications. For details, contact the Special Sales Department, Sky Pony Press, 307 West 36th Street, 11th Floor, New York, NY 10018 or info@skyhorsepublishing.com.

Sky Pony® is a registered trademark of Skyhorse Publishing, Inc.®, a Delaware corporation.

Visit our website at www.skyponypress.com.

10 9 8 7 6 5 4 3 2 1

Manufactured in China, 2021
This product conforms to CPSIA 2008

Library of Congress Cataloging-in-Publication Data is available on file.

Cover design by David Ter-Avanesyan

Print ISBN: 978-1-5107-6691-4

Contents

How to Solve the Puzzles

Sudoku Example

				1	2
3					
			4	5	
	4	1			
					6
4	2				

6	5	4	3	1	2
3	1	2	5	6	4
2	6	3	4	5	1
5	4	1	6	2	3
1	3	5	2	4	6
4	2	6	1	3	5

Sudoku has become a popular puzzle around the world! Place numbers into the grid so that each row, column, and bold outlined box has the digits, in this example, from 1–6 (although puzzles may go up to 8 in this book). Digits cannot repeat in a row, column, or bold outlined box.

The main questions to ask when you solve a sudoku:

- Where can the number __ go in a row/column/box?
- What numbers can be in a specific square?

To start in this example, we can look in row 1. Where can we place the 3? It can't be in the first three columns, as those share the box with the 3 in row 2. Thus, we can place the 3 in row 1, column 4 (R1C4 for short). Similarly, for the 1 in row 2, we can't place it in columns 4–6 (shares a box with the 1 in R1C5), nor can we place it in column 3 (shares the column with the 1 in R4C3). Therefore, we place the 1 in R2C2 and a 2 in R2C3.

Now let's look at row 6, column 5. What numbers can be in that square? It can't be 1 or 5 (in the same column), 2 or 4 (same row), or 6 (same box). That leaves 3 as the only possibility there!

Using this logic, we can continue to place the rest of the numbers on the right side, and then move to the left to complete the solution.

Some sudoku puzzles can have much harder logic than this. The puzzles in this book are all solvable without using harder logic (and are solvable without guessing), but if you know those techniques, feel free to use them!

Encrypted Questions Example

J MPWF ZPV. → I LOVE YOU.

The Encrypted Questions puzzles in this book use a type of encoding called a shift cipher (or a Caesar cipher). In order to encode the message, we take each letter and move it forward a certain number of places in the alphabet. In the example above, this means we take the I and replace it with J, we take the L and replace it with M, etc. If we go past the end of the alphabet, we go back to the beginning of the alphabet, so Z→A.

To decode one of these messages, we simply move backwards the same number of letters. In the above case, we move from J back to I, M back to L, and so on, to recover the original message of "I LOVE YOU." Again, if we go past the beginning of the alphabet that way, we wrap back to Z.

A tricky thing can happen if you don't know how many letters the message has been shifted. The best strategy then is to try to find common words that you can change the word into. For example, if you see a one-letter word, it's probably either "A" or "I." Similarly, other common words may include "the," "he," "she," or "to." You can try to find words in the list that match these, and see if the rest of the message makes sense!

Pyramid Example

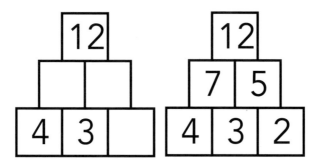

In the pyramid puzzles, your job is to reconstruct the number pyramid, using the given numbers. Each number is the sum of the two numbers directly under it. To solve the puzzle, you need to be able to climb up or down the pyramid to figure out all the numbers.

Let's start in the second row. The box above the 4 and 3 must be their sum, so in this case, we can write the number 7 in there. Now let's look at the 12. It must be the sum of the two numbers beneath it, one of which is 7. So we ask: What plus 7 equals 12? The answer is 5, so we can write the 5 in the second box in row 2. We can do the same thing for the final square in row 3. 5 − 3 = 2, so we write 2 in the bottom right corner.

Puzzles

Sudoku 1

Enter all the digits from 1–6 in each box, such that no digit repeats in each row, column, or box.

1	2				
				3	
		2			4
3			5		
	4				
				6	1

Sudoku 2

Enter all the digits from 1–6 in each box, such that no digit repeats in each row, column, or box.

		2	3		
	4			5	
2					3
1					4
	2			6	
		5	1		

Sudoku 3

Enter all the digits from 1–6 in each box, such that no digit repeats in each row, column, or box.

1			3		
	2			1	
		3			2
5			4		
	4			5	
		5			6

Sudoku 4

Enter all the digits from 1–6 in each box, such that no digit repeats in each row, column, or box.

4		5	6		1
5	3			4	6
		2	3		
	6			5	
		3	4		

Sudoku 5

Enter all the digits from 1–6 in each box, such that no digit repeats in each row, column, or box.

2					4
	4			2	
		6	4		
		5	1		
	5			3	
1					5

Sudoku 6

Enter all the digits from 1–6 in each box, such that no digit repeats in each row, column, or box.

5			4		
1			6		
	6			1	
	2			3	
		4			5
		3			2

Sudoku 7

Enter all the digits from 1–6 in each box, such that no digit repeats in each row, column, or box.

1		3			
	2				3
		2		5	
	6		3		
3				2	
			1		4

Sudoku 8

Enter all the digits from 1–6 in each box, such that no digit repeats in each row, column, or box.

1		2		5	
			3		
	2				1
5				4	
		3			
	1		4		5

Sudoku 9

Enter all the digits from 1–8 in each box, such that no digit repeats in each row, column, or box. (This might seem harder, but it can be solved using the same techniques used in the previous puzzles!)

7			4	5			1
		3			6		
	2					7	
1			5	3			8
8			3	6			4
	1					5	
		1			3		
6			2	4			7

Sudoku 10

Enter all the digits from 1–8 in each box, such that no digit repeats in each row, column, or box.

1		5				6	
	2				7		5
	6		4				
7				2		1	
	3		2				7
				3		2	
6		7				3	
	8				6		1

Word Search 1

If you like animals with short names, you're in luck! There are 25 three-letter words hidden in the grid below. Can you find them all?

```
O P O U C B O A L D
F L Y K T A L O H S
T O O C H T L W O M
E E X Y P E M U G A
E C L A E I N A A P
Y A K B D O G N U E
A T N C D E U S M P
A X C T K E N A S D
K U C O W N R A T O
E L K E D S A H T E
```

ANT	DOE	HEN
APE	DOG	HOG
ASP	EEL	OWL
BAT	ELK	PIG
BEE	EMU	RAM
BOA	EWE	RAT
CAT	FLY	YAK
COD	FOX	
COW	GNU	

Word Search 2

There are a lot of colors in the world. Find many of them hidden in the grid below, and add some color to your day!

```
K  L  I  M  E  D  C  Y  A  N
R  N  A  T  A  E  T  E  A  L
C  H  I  Y  A  R  G  B  E  N
E  H  N  P  B  R  O  W  N  A
W  T  D  E  T  E  L  O  I  V
B  E  I  G  E  R  D  L  N  Y
L  E  G  G  L  R  B  L  U  E
A  T  O  R  A  N  G  E  I  S
C  R  E  V  L  I  S  Y  G  O
K  M  A  G  E  N  T  A  I  R
```

BEIGE	INDIGO	ROSE
BLACK	LIME	SILVER
BLUE	MAGENTA	TAN
BROWN	MAROON	TEAL
CYAN	NAVY	VIOLET
GOLD	ORANGE	WHITE
GRAY	PINK	YELLOW
GREEN	RED	

Word Search 3

You'll have to plan it out very carefully to find these planets and other objects found in the solar system!

```
E N U T P E N P P C
U I E A U L R O S A
R M I O H E U H D L
O E N S T U T T I L
P R O I A R A I O I
A C P R A A S T R S
S U N E V N E A E T
J R R D A U R N T O
C Y A T O S E T S E
N O O M P H C R A T
```

ASTEROID	JUPITER	SATURN
CALLISTO	MARS	TITAN
CERES	MERCURY	URANUS
EARTH	MOON	VENUS
ERIS	NEPTUNE	
EUROPA	PLUTO	

Word Search 4

Looking for a sweet treat? You can find a number of desserts and other sweets here!

```
T W E G D U F R U I T I
P T A O G E L A T O E N
U E C U S T A R D R I R
M L S F E K N D E L P S
P U D D I N G I O N Y S
K E I C K L N N E E R U
I S K W O W N E A W R N
N E E A O A T O R T E D
P S I R C E L P P A H A
I T B Y O E R I A L C E
E N O L E M R E T A W F
E L F F U O S C O N E G
```

APPLE CRISP	**ECLAIR**	**SCONE**
BROWNIE	**FLAN**	**SMORES**
CAKE	**FRUIT**	**SOUFFLE**
CANNOLI	**FUDGE**	**SUNDAE**
CHERRY PIE	**GELATO**	**TORTE**
COOKIES	**PUDDING**	**WATERMELON**
CUSTARD	**PUMPKIN PIE**	

Word Search 5

If you're looking to sport a new look, you should be able to find some fun sports hidden below!

```
N  S  W  I  M  M  I  N  G  W  L  N
L  B  I  S  C  R  I  C  K  E  T  O
L  B  G  U  E  Y  S  I  N  N  E  T
A  A  W  R  S  O  C  C  E  R  C  N
B  S  A  F  F  L  I  L  B  B  N  I
Y  K  T  I  O  U  T  A  I  E  R  M
E  E  E  N  O  G  S  A  G  N  U  D
L  T  R  G  T  E  A  G  N  T  G  A
L  B  P  O  B  A  N  T  I  R  B  B
O  A  O  A  A  A  M  N  I  I  Y  N
V  L  L  L  L  Y  E  K  C  O  H
A  L  O  F  L  O  G  G  S  G  R  G
```

BADMINTON	GOLF	SOCCER
BASEBALL	GYMNASTICS	SURFING
BASKETBALL	HOCKEY	SWIMMING
CRICKET	LUGE	TENNIS
CYCLING	RUGBY	VOLLEYBALL
FOOTBALL	SKIING	WATER POLO

Word Search 6

Solve the equations, and then find the answers spelled out in the grid below!

```
F  Y  T  H  I  R  T  Y  V  E
I  T  Y  N  Y  T  N  E  W  T
F  I  F  T  E  E  N  E  V  W
T  V  E  H  E  W  E  L  S  E
Y  O  S  I  X  R  F  E  E  L
S  N  W  R  H  N  W  V  N  V
W  E  U  T  H  G  I  E  H  E
O  O  V  E  O  F  T  N  E  E
F  I  Z  E  R  O  E  U  E  O
E  N  V  N  N  Y  T  R  O  F
```

14-6	16-7	12-9
3+8	4-3	4+8
9+6	5+2	4x5
10x5	2+4	8-6
12-7	8+2	7-7
8x5	11+2	
7-3	3x10	

Word Search 7

This is a unique puzzle. Hidden in the grid below is exactly one copy of the word "unique." Can you find it hidden in there?

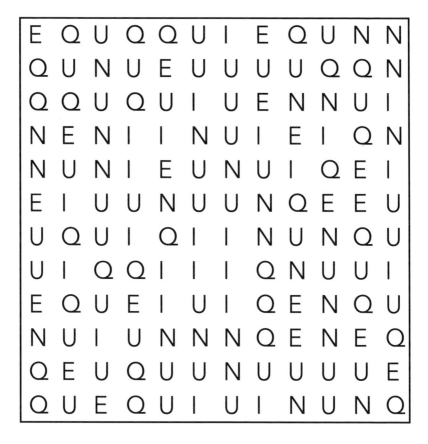

```
E Q U Q Q U I E Q U N N
Q U N U E U U U U Q Q N
Q Q U Q U I U E N N U I
N E N I I N U I E I Q N
N U N I E U N U I Q E I
E I U U N U U N Q E E U
U Q U I Q I I N U N Q U
U I Q Q I I I Q N U U I
E Q U E I U I Q E N Q U
N U I U N N N Q E N E Q
Q E U Q U U N U U U U E
Q U E Q U I U I N U N Q
```

UNIQUE

Word Search 8

The first thirteen states in the United States are listed below the grid. Their capital cities are hidden in the grid below. It would be a capital idea to find them!

```
D N O S I D A M B G D E
E G D R O C N O C R R P
R S M E L A S N A U R R
A T N A L T A T I B B O
L R E V O D S P Y S D V
E E C N E U T E N I N I
I V A B G R R L A R O D
G N O U U M E I B R M E
H E A E O T N E L A H N
O D D R O F T R A H C C
A I B M U L O C I E I E
S I L O P A N N A E R R
```

CONNECTICUT   **NEW HAMPSHIRE**   **PENNSYLVANIA**
DELAWARE   **NEW JERSEY**   **RHODE ISLAND**
GEORGIA   **NEW YORK**   **SOUTH CAROLINA**
MARYLAND   **NORTH**   **VIRGINIA**
MASSACHUSETTS   **CAROLINA**

Word Search 9

They say it's hard to find a needle in a haystack, but can you find the single copy of the word "NEEDLE" hidden in the grid below?

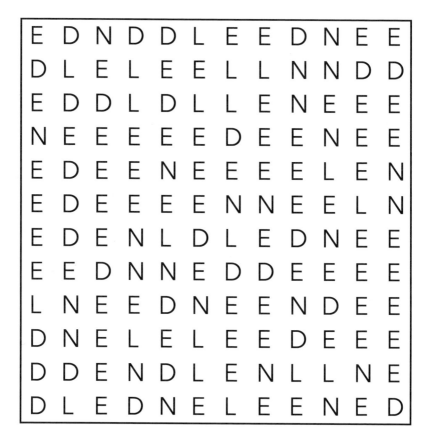

```
E D N D D L E E D N E E
D L E L E E L L N N D D
E D D L D L L E N E E E
N E E E E E D E E N E E
E D E E N E E E E L E N
E D E E E E N N E E L N
E D E N L D L E D N E E
E E D N N E D D E E E E
L N E E D N E E N D E E
D N E L E L E E D E E E
D D E N D L E N L L N E
D L E D N E L E E N E D
```

NEEDLE

Word Clouds 1

The following nine clouds have a common theme to them. However, each of the clouds are scrambled! Unscramble the letters in each cloud, and then identify the theme!

If you need a hint, you can check out the Hints section to find the common theme.

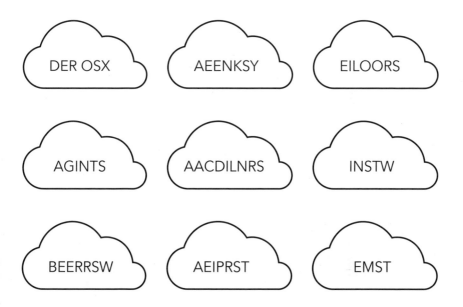

Word Clouds 2

The following nine clouds have a common theme to them. However, each of the clouds are scrambled! Unscramble the letters in each cloud, and then identify the theme!

   If you need a hint, you can check out the Hints section to find the common theme.

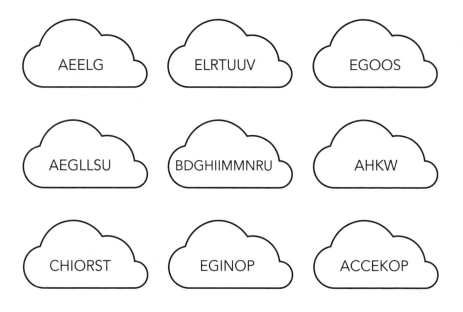

Word Clouds 3

The following nine clouds have a common theme to them. However, each of the clouds are scrambled! Unscramble the letters in each cloud, and then identify the theme!

If you need a hint, you can check out the Hints section to find the common theme.

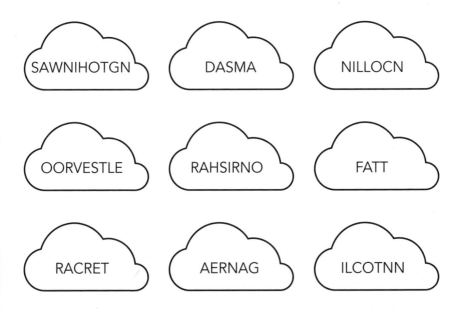

SAWNIHOTGN

DASMA

NILLOCN

OORVESTLE

RAHSIRNO

FATT

RACRET

AERNAG

ILCOTNN

Word Clouds 4

The following nine clouds have a common theme to them. However, each of the clouds are scrambled! Unscramble the letters in each cloud, and then identify the theme!

If you need a hint, you can check out the Hints section to find the common theme.

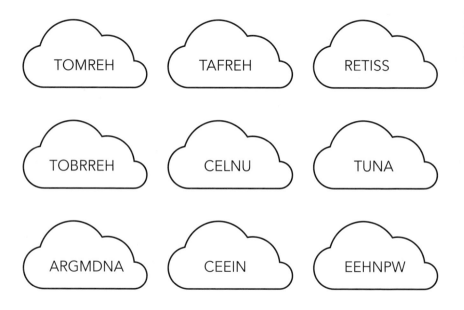

TOMREH

TAFREH

RETISS

TOBRREH

CELNU

TUNA

ARGMDNA

CEEIN

EEHNPW

Word Clouds 5

The following nine clouds have a common theme to them. However, each of the clouds are scrambled! Unscramble the letters in each cloud, and then identify the theme!

If you need a hint, you can check out the Hints section to find the common theme.

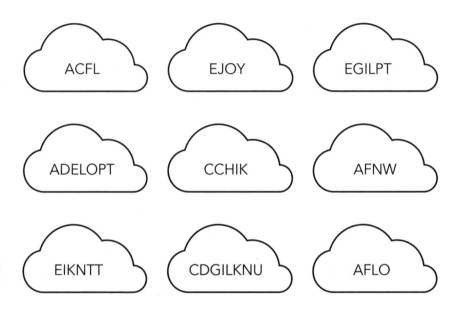

ACFL

EJOY

EGILPT

ADELOPT

CCHIK

AFNW

EIKNTT

CDGILKNU

AFLO

Word Clouds 6

The following nine clouds have a common theme to them. However, each of the clouds are scrambled! Unscramble the letters in each cloud, and then identify the theme!

    If you need a hint, you can check out the Hints section to find the common theme.

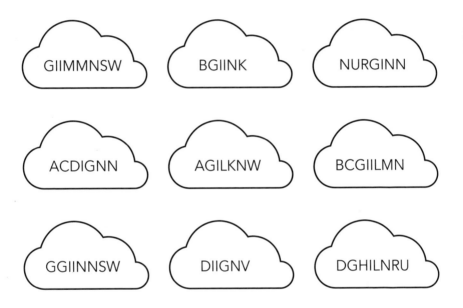

GIIMMNSW

BGIINK

NURGINN

ACDIGNN

AGILKNW

BCGIILMN

GGIINNSW

DIIGNV

DGHILNRU

Word Clouds 7

The following nine clouds have a common theme to them. However, each of the clouds are scrambled! Unscramble the letters in each cloud, and then identify the theme!

   If you need a hint, you can check out the Hints section to find the common theme.

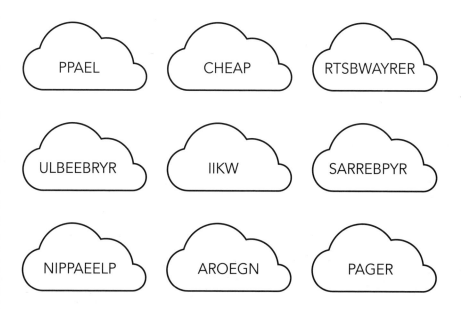

PPAEL

CHEAP

RTSBWAYRER

ULBEEBRYR

IIKW

SARREBPYR

NIPPAEELP

AROEGN

PAGER

Hidden Words 1

The following paragraph has three animal names hidden in the text. Look carefully to find where they are hidden! Note that the letters will appear in order, but may be split between words or lines. (As an example: "I had to sh<u>ow</u> <u>l</u>ast week's pictures to my friends.")

I went to the field to scatter some tree seeds. The nearby trees gave a lot of shade, making the temperature nice and cool. My phone rang; I got terrible news and realized that I had to leave early. With a scowl on my face, I left and stomped back to my car.

Hidden Words 2

The following paragraph has three animal names hidden in the text. Look carefully to find where they are hidden! Note that the letters will appear in order, but may be split between words or lines. (As an example: "I had to sh**ow** **l**ast week's pictures to my friends.")

The girl peeled her banana, as she was absolutely famished. She looked at the leftover calamari and shuddered. "I abhor seafood. Give me a special treat any day!" Her mother relented and let her have some chicken nuggets.

Hidden Words 3

The following paragraph has three country names hidden in the text. Look carefully to find where they are hidden! Note that the letters will appear in order, but may be split between words or lines. (As in the example with animals: "I had to sh<u>ow l</u>ast week's pictures to my friends.")

"Ouch! That was painful!" Bobby said, as he rubbed his arm. "I ran from one side of the park to the other, but tripped on a branch, bumped my chin, and then skinned my knee!" Fortunately, his mother had a bandage, and he was soon playing on the slides.

Hidden Words 4

The following paragraph has three country names hidden in the text. Look carefully to find where they are hidden! Note that the letters will appear in order, but may be split between words or lines. (As in the example with animals: "I had to sh<u>ow l</u>ast week's pictures to my friends.")

The plane began its descent into the airport. "I find I am not a fan of airplanes," complained the man seated on my left. "I tend to mope, ruminating about all the horror stories that I've heard." Despite his repeated complaints, it turned out to be a nice landing.

Hidden Words 5

The following paragraph has three state names hidden in the text. Look carefully to find where they are hidden! Note that the letters will appear in order, but may be split between words or lines. (As in the example with animals: "I had to sh<u>ow l</u>ast week's pictures to my friends.")

It was a foregone conclusion. The children had gone crazy, making a giant mess of the playroom. "We want the kids to remain engaged, instead of getting distracted," said the babysitter. "Hey kids! Let's go color a dog in your coloring books!"

Hidden Words 6

The following paragraph has three state names hidden in the text. Look carefully to find where they are hidden! Note that the letters will appear in order, but may be split between words or lines. (As in the example with animals: "I had to sh<u>ow l</u>ast week's pictures to my friends.")

> The children were playing hide and seek with their toys. "I hid a horse behind the couch," said Hal. "Ask Andy where he hid the monkey. I'll put a hippo under the table!"

Hidden Words 7

The following paragraph has three vehicles hidden in the text. Look carefully to find where they are hidden!
Note that the letters will appear in order, but may be split between words or lines. (As in the example with animals: "I had to sh<u>ow l</u>ast week's pictures to my friends.")

Sally strained as she tried to reach the remote control. "My plan entailed watching a police movie, but Dad didn't care at all for that choice, so now I have to watch the baseball game."

Hidden Words 8

The following paragraph has three vehicles hidden in the text. Look carefully to find where they are hidden!
Note that the letters will appear in order, but may be split between words or lines. (As in the example with animals: "I had to sh<u>ow l</u>ast week's pictures to my friends.")

"Did you hear the news?" I asked as I struck up a conversation with the zookeeper. "I heard they needed to move the boa to a different exhibit, and I'll never see it ever again!" The zookeeper assured me that it would return soon, and certainly was not going to vanish.

Hidden Words 9

The following paragraph has three beverages hidden in the text. Look carefully to find where they are hidden!
Note that the letters will appear in order, but may be split between words or lines. (As in the example with animals: "I had to sh**ow l**ast week's pictures to my friends.")

I sat back, looking at the page in the coloring book. I took the teal crayon so I could color in the sky. I tried to swat errant flies that landed near me. Unfortunately, a mosquito bit my arm as I shooed the fly, so Dad had to put a bandage on it.

Hidden Words 10

The following paragraph has three kinds of food hidden in the text. Look carefully to find where they are hidden! Note that the letters will appear in order, but may be split between words or lines. (As in the example with animals: "I had to sh<u>ow l</u>ast week's pictures to my friends.")

"You need to take a nap, please," said Mom, as she folded the laundry. "You've been a bit cranky, and I can tell you're tired. Don't look at me that way; you're exhausted! Before you go upstairs, could you please bring me the clothes from the hamper? When you wake up, you will be a new kid!"

Hidden Words 11

The following paragraph has three kinds of mythical creatures hidden in the text. Look carefully to find where they are hidden! Note that the letters will appear in order, but may be split between words or lines. (As in the example with animals: "I had to sh<u>ow l</u>ast week's pictures to my friends.")

"This art program is very easy to use," said Peggy. "To color the picture, use the mouse to drag onto the canvas. If you take your time, you should be able to sketch a fair young puppy. After you watch me do it, you'll easily be able to do it yourself!"

Encrypted Questions 1

A question and answer have been encoded below using a Caesar cipher. Can you decrypt the message to figure out this riddle?

To help you practice, we'll give you a hint! To decode this message, shift each letter one letter forward in the alphabet (for example, A→B, B→C).

VGX CHC SGD RJDKDSNM CDBHCD MNS SN FN SN SGD CZMBD?

HS GZC MN ANCX SN CZMBD VHSG.

A	B	C	D	E	F	G	H	I	J	K	L	M

N	O	P	Q	R	S	T	U	V	W	X	Y	Z

Encrypted Questions 2

A question and answer have been encoded below using a Caesar cipher. Can you decrypt the message to figure out this riddle?

To help you practice, we'll give you a hint! To decode this message, shift each letter one letter forward in the alphabet (for example, A→B, B→C).

CHC XNT GDZQ SGD INJD ZANTS SGD SGQDD GNKDR HM SGD FQNTMC?

VDKK . . . VDKK . . . VDKK . . .

A	B	C	D	E	F	G	H	I	J	K	L	M
N	O	P	Q	R	S	T	U	V	W	X	Y	Z

Encrypted Questions 3

A question and answer have been encoded below using a Caesar cipher. Can you decrypt the message to figure out this riddle?

To help you practice, we'll give you a hint! To decode this message, shift each letter one letter backward in the alphabet (for example, B→A, C→B).

EJE ZPV IFBS UIF KPLF BCPVU UIF KVNQ SPQF?

JU'T UPP MPOH. MFU'T KVTU TLJQ JU.

A	B	C	D	E	F	G	H	I	J	K	L	M
N	O	P	Q	R	S	T	U	V	W	X	Y	Z

Encrypted Questions 4

A question and answer have been encoded below using a Caesar cipher. Can you decrypt the message to figure out this riddle?

 To help you practice, we'll give you a hint! To decode this message, shift each letter one letter backward in the alphabet (for example, B→A, C→B).

XIZ EP QFPQMF IFBS NVTJD QMBZJOH CBDLXBSET BU
CFFUIPWFO'T HSBWF?

IF JT EFDPNQPTJOH.

A	B	C	D	E	F	G	H	I	J	K	L	M
N	O	P	Q	R	S	T	U	V	W	X	Y	Z

Encrypted Questions 5

A question and answer have been encoded below using a Caesar cipher. Can you decrypt the message to figure out this riddle?

This message has shifted each letter by one. However, I forgot whether the shift is forward or backward! It's up to you to figure it out! Remember to look for common words like "a" or "the" to help you out. (If you need to find out the shift, check out the Hints section.)

XIBU EJE UIF EJWFST GJOE TIBLJOH BU UIF CPUUPN PG UIF PDFBO?

B OFSWPVT XSFDL.

A	B	C	D	E	F	G	H	I	J	K	L	M

N	O	P	Q	R	S	T	U	V	W	X	Y	Z

Encrypted Questions 6

A question and answer have been encoded below using a Caesar cipher. Can you decrypt the message to figure out this riddle?

   This message has shifted each letter by one. However, I forgot whether the shift is forward or backward! It's up to you to figure it out! Remember to look for common words like "a" or "the" to help you out. (If you need to find out the shift, check out the Hints section.)

VGX VZR SGD EZQLDQ'R RNM RGZJHMF SGD BNVR?

GD VZMSDC Z LHKJRGZJD.

A	B	C	D	E	F	G	H	I	J	K	L	M
N	O	P	Q	R	S	T	U	V	W	X	Y	Z

Encrypted Questions 7

A question and answer have been encoded below using a Caesar cipher. Can you decrypt the message to figure out this riddle?

    This message has shifted each letter by one. However, I forgot whether the shift is forward or backward! It's up to you to figure it out! Remember to look for common words like "a" or "the" to help you out. (If you need to find out the shift, check out the Hints section.)

GNV CHC SGD BNNJHD EDDK VGDM HS VNJD TO?

BGHO-ODQ.

A	B	C	D	E	F	G	H	I	J	K	L	M
N	O	P	Q	R	S	T	U	V	W	X	Y	Z

Encrypted Questions 8

A question and answer have been encoded below using a Caesar cipher. Can you decrypt the message to figure out this riddle?

This message has shifted each letter by one. However, I forgot whether the shift is forward or backward! It's up to you to figure it out! Remember to look for common words like "a" or "the" to help you out. (If you need to find out the shift, check out the Hints section.)

XIZ DPVMEO'U UIF QJSBUF SFDJUF UIF BMQIBCFU?

IF BMXBZT HPU MPTU BU D.

A	B	C	D	E	F	G	H	I	J	K	L	M
N	O	P	Q	R	S	T	U	V	W	X	Y	Z

Encrypted Questions 9

A question and answer have been encoded below using a Caesar cipher. Can you decrypt the message to figure out this riddle?

From here on, it's up to you to figure out how to shift the cipher to find the message. Remember that all letters will be shifted by the same number of letters, and that common words will help you break the code! (If you need to find out the shift, check out the Hints section.)

YJCV UQWPF FQGU C UNGGRKPI VTKEGTCVQRU OCMG?

C FKPQ-UPQTG

A	B	C	D	E	F	G	H	I	J	K	L	M
N	O	P	Q	R	S	T	U	V	W	X	Y	Z

Encrypted Questions 10

A question and answer have been encoded below using a Caesar cipher. Can you decrypt the message to figure out this riddle? (If you need to find out the shift, check out the Hints section.)

VGZS CHC SGD BKNTC VDZQ TMCDQ HSR RGNQSR?

SGTMCDQVDZQ.

A	B	C	D	E	F	G	H	I	J	K	L	M
N	O	P	Q	R	S	T	U	V	W	X	Y	Z

Encrypted Questions 11

A question and answer have been encoded below using a Caesar cipher. Can you decrypt the message to figure out this riddle? (If you need to find out the shift, check out the Hints section.)

UFYR BGB RFC MACYL QYW RM RFC ZCYAF?

LMRFGLE. GR HSQR UYTCB.

A	B	C	D	E	F	G	H	I	J	K	L	M
N	O	P	Q	R	S	T	U	V	W	X	Y	Z

Encrypted Questions 12

A question and answer have been encoded below using a Caesar cipher. Can you decrypt the message to figure out this riddle? (If you need to find out the shift, check out the Hints section.)

TEXQ FP X ZXQ'P CXSLOFQB ZLILO?

MROO-MIB.

A	B	C	D	E	F	G	H	I	J	K	L	M
N	O	P	Q	R	S	T	U	V	W	X	Y	Z

Encrypted Questions 13

A question and answer have been encoded below using a Caesar cipher. Can you decrypt the message to figure out this riddle? (If you need to find out the shift, check out the Hints section.)

ALIVI HS CSY PIEVR LSA XS QEOI E FERERE WTPMX?

WYRHEI WGLSSP

A	B	C	D	E	F	G	H	I	J	K	L	M
N	O	P	Q	R	S	T	U	V	W	X	Y	Z

Encrypted Questions 14

A question and answer have been encoded below using a Caesar cipher. Can you decrypt the message to figure out this riddle? (If you need to find out the shift, check out the Hints section.)

G YQICB KW BME GD QFC AMSJB RCJJ KC UFYR DMSP KGLSQ DMSP GQ.

QFC QYGB LMRFGLE.

A	B	C	D	E	F	G	H	I	J	K	L	M
N	O	P	Q	R	S	T	U	V	W	X	Y	Z

Encrypted Questions 15

A statement and response have been encoded below using a Caesar cipher. Can you decrypt the message to figure out this riddle? (If you need to find out the shift, check out the Hints section.)

NZ EBE TBJE UIF NBUI KPLFT IF UFMMT NF BSFO'U BMM CBE.

KVTU TVN BSF.

A	B	C	D	E	F	G	H	I	J	K	L	M
N	O	P	Q	R	S	T	U	V	W	X	Y	Z

Pyramid 1

A number pyramid is shown below. The number in each box is the sum of the two numbers in the boxes directly underneath it. Based on the given numbers, can you figure out the remaining numbers?

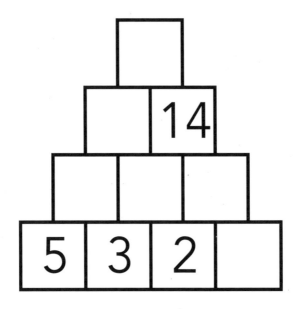

Pyramid 2

A number pyramid is shown below. The number in each box is the sum of the two numbers in the boxes directly underneath it. Based on the given numbers, can you figure out the remaining numbers?

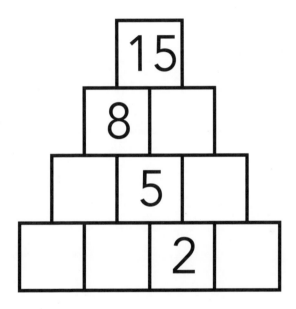

Pyramid 3

A number pyramid is shown below. The number in each box is the sum of the two numbers in the boxes directly underneath it. Based on the given numbers, can you figure out the remaining numbers?

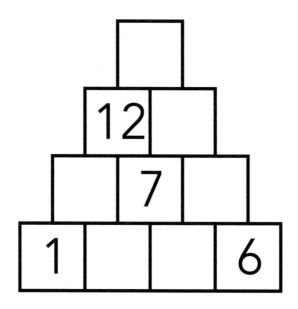

Pyramid 4

A number pyramid is shown below. The number in each box is the sum of the two numbers in the boxes directly underneath it. Based on the given numbers, can you figure out the remaining numbers?

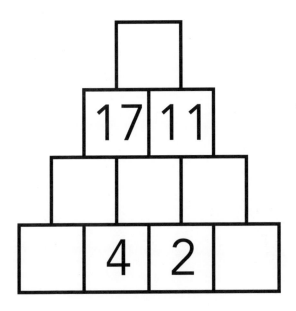

Pyramid 5

A number pyramid is shown below. The number in each box is the sum of the two numbers in the boxes directly underneath it. Based on the given numbers, can you figure out the remaining numbers?

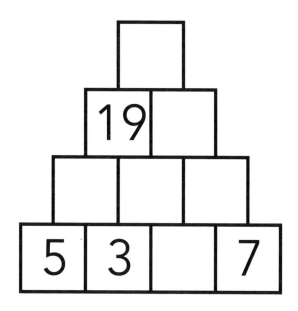

Pyramid 6

A number pyramid is shown below. The number in each box is the sum of the two numbers in the boxes directly underneath it. Based on the given numbers, can you figure out the remaining numbers?

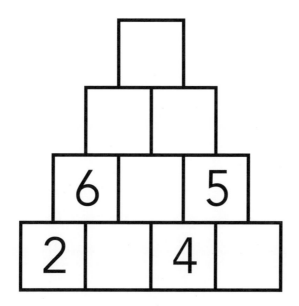

Pyramid 7

A number pyramid is shown below. The number in each box is the sum of the two numbers in the boxes directly underneath it. Based on the given numbers, can you figure out the remaining numbers?

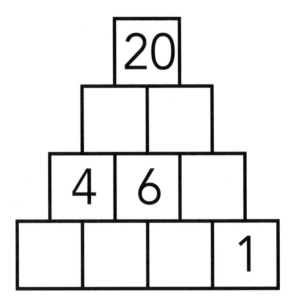

Pyramid 8

A number pyramid is shown below. The number in each box is the sum of the two numbers in the boxes directly underneath it. Based on the given numbers, can you figure out the remaining numbers?

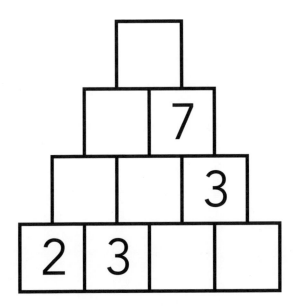

Pyramid 9

A number pyramid is shown below. The number in each box is the sum of the two numbers in the boxes directly underneath it. Based on the given numbers, can you figure out the remaining numbers?

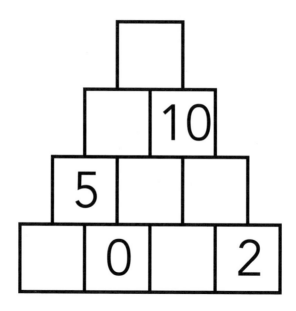

Pyramid 10

A number pyramid is shown below. The number in each box is the sum of the two numbers in the boxes directly underneath it. Based on the given numbers, can you figure out the remaining numbers?

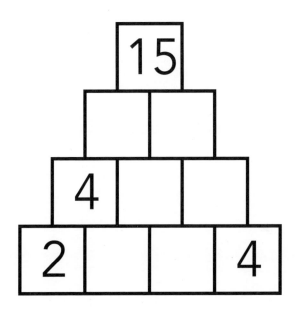

Spot the Same 1

In the grid below, exactly two of the boxes have the same contents (ignoring the letters, which are used in the answer key). Can you find the two boxes that are identical?

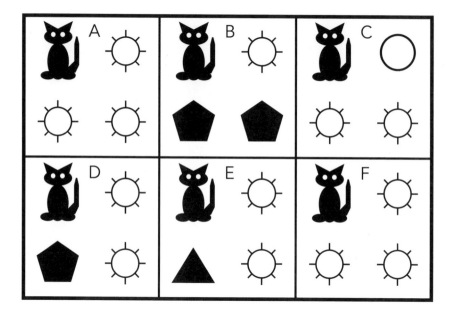

Spot the Same 2

In the grid below, exactly two of the boxes have the same contents (ignoring the letters, which are used in the answer key). Can you find the two boxes that are identical?

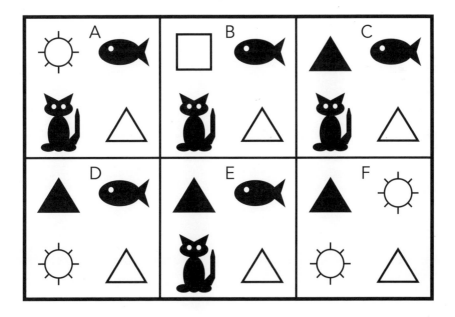

Spot the Same 3

In the grid below, exactly two of the boxes have the same contents (ignoring the letters, which are used in the answer key). Can you find the two boxes that are identical?

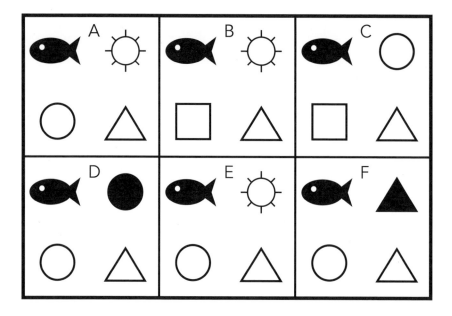

Spot the Same 4

In the grid below, exactly two of the boxes have the same contents (ignoring the letters, which are used in the answer key). Can you find the two boxes that are identical?

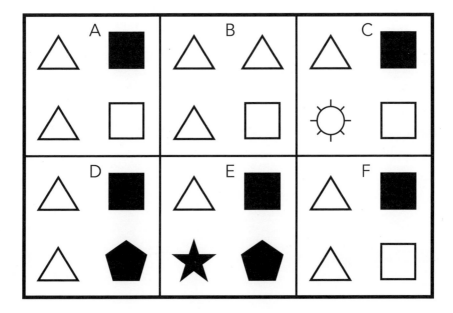

Spot the Same 5

In the grid below, exactly two of the boxes have the same contents (ignoring the letters, which are used in the answer key). Can you find the two boxes that are identical?

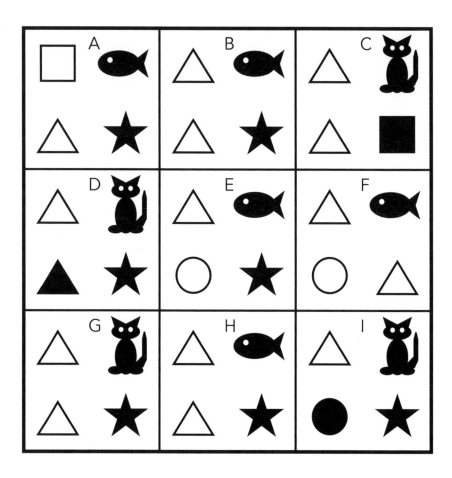

Spot the Same 6

In the grid below, exactly two of the boxes have the same contents (ignoring the letters, which are used in the answer key). Can you find the two boxes that are identical?

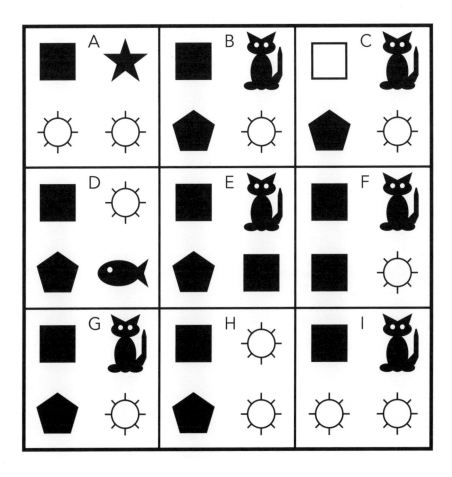

Spot the Same 7

In the grid below, exactly two of the boxes have the same contents (ignoring the letters, which are used in the answer key). Can you find the two boxes that are identical?

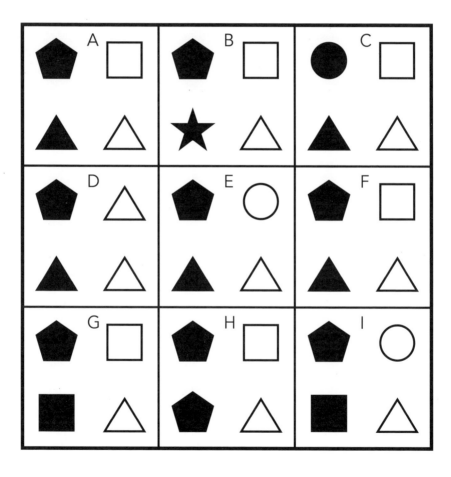

Spot the Same 8

In the grid below, exactly two of the boxes have the same contents (ignoring the letters, which are used in the answer key). Can you find the two boxes that are identical?

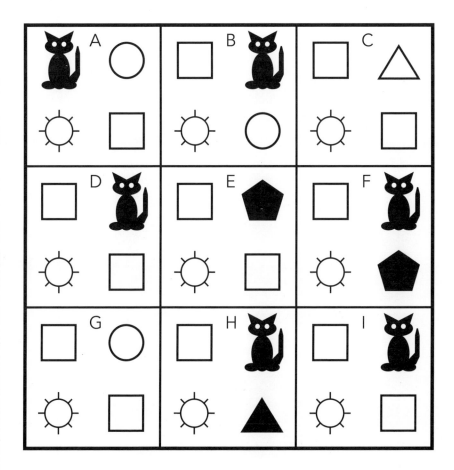

Spot the Same 9

In the grid below, exactly two of the boxes have the same contents (ignoring the letters, which are used in the answer key). Can you find the two boxes that are identical?

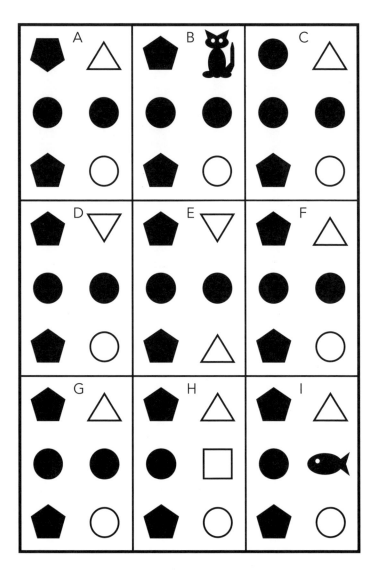

Spot the Same 10

In the grid below, exactly two of the boxes have the same contents (ignoring the letters, which are used in the answer key). Can you find the two boxes that are identical?

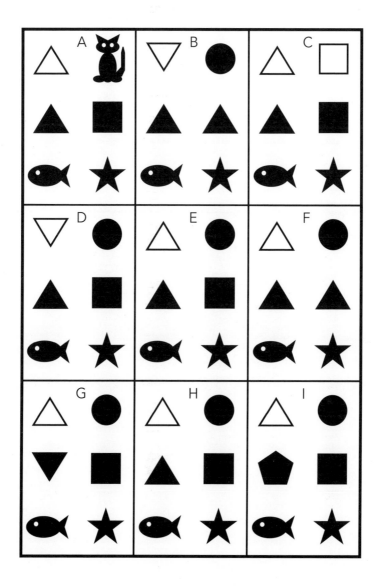

Logic Puzzle 1

On the planet of Ancalagon, it was common for each resident to have their own pet dragon. Molly and her four best friends all had dragons, and strangely, each dragon was a different color. Using the following clues, can you figure out what color dragon each child had?

1. The names of two children started with the same letter as the color of their dragon.
2. Robert didn't have a blue dragon.
3. Susan and the child with the green dragon often would let their dragons play together during the morning.
4. Barbara was not the child with the black dragon.

	Black	Blue	Green	Red	White
Barbara					
Charlie					
Molly					
Robert					
Susan					

Logic Puzzle 2

Al and his four friends participated in a 5K race last week. Based on the following clues, can you figure out the order in which each competitor finished?

1. Billy finished faster than Connie, but slower than Elizabeth.
2. David finished in third place.
3. The position in which Al finished was an even number.
4. Billy took an early lead, but David passed him at the 3K mark, and Billy never caught back up.

	1st	2nd	3rd	4th	5th
Al					
Billy					
Connie					
David					
Elizabeth					

Logic Puzzle 3

A new exhibit opened up at the local aquarium, and Nora and her four friends went to visit. The aquarium had five brand new exhibits, and each friend loved a different exhibit. Using the following clues, can you deduce what animal each friend enjoyed the most on their visit?

1. Polly and the boy who likes the crab drove to the aquarium in the same car.
2. Robert's and Marian's favorites were, in some order, the whale and the flounder.
3. Neither Nora nor the girl who liked the whales enjoyed the shark exhibit.
4. Sebastian was not a huge fan of the manatee exhibit.

	Crab	Flounder	Manatee	Shark	Whale
Marian					
Nora					
Polly					
Robert					
Sebastian					

Logic Puzzle 4

Six classmates at Learning View Academy were talking at lunch one day about their favorite subjects. Each student had a different subject that was their absolute favorite. Using the following clues, can you figure out each student's favorite school subject (one of which was physical education)?

1. At least two students like a class that starts with the same letter as their name.
2. Gail prefers either French or English.
3. Evan and the boy who likes geometry take the same bus home every day.
4. Buddy did not like any of his math classes.
5. Frank was not a fan of science, and really didn't like chemistry.
6. Deb often tutored the brother of the student whose favorite subject was history.

	Chemistry	English	French	Geometry	History	Phys. Ed.
Buddy						
Cindy						
Deb						
Evan						
Frank						
Gail						

Logic Puzzle 5

Caroline and her four friends get together every Saturday morning to watch their favorite TV shows. Fortunately, each child's favorite show comes on at a different time (every half hour from 9:00 a.m. until 11:00 a.m.), and each child's favorite show is based around a different animal. Based on the following clues, can you determine each child's favorite animal, and the time that the show airs?

1. Annie's favorite show started earlier than the show that starred the horse.
2. Ezekiel's show started at 10:00 a.m.
3. The show starring the pig was the final show that the children watched, starting at 11:00 a.m.
4. Dawn's favorite show starred Ricky the Rooster.
5. Brenda loved the show starring the giraffe. That show aired after the show starring the horse.
6. The rooster's show was the first show, airing at 9:00 a.m.

	9:00 a.m.	9:30 a.m.	10:00 a.m.	10:30 a.m.	11:00 a.m.	Cow	Giraffe	Horse	Pig	Rooster
Annie										
Brenda										
Caroline										
Dawn										
Ezekiel										
Cow										
Giraffe										
Horse										
Pig										
Rooster										

Logic Puzzle 6

After watching the recent Olympics, Sandra and her five friends were all inspired to start training on the sports that they had watched. Each friend was inspired to train for a different event (which included basketball, diving, gymnastics, swimming, triathlon, and track & field). Given the following clues, can you determine which event each person played?

1. No person's favorite sport starts with the same letter as the first letter of their name.
2. Gina prefers a sport that involves a pool; even though the triathlon involves swimming, she doesn't like biking, so she didn't train in that.
3. Barbara would carpool to her practice with the person who was training in track & field.
4. Tony and the person training for basketball would meet after practice for ice cream.
5. At least one person's favorite sport starts with the last letter of their name.
6. David is not a fan of basketball.

	Basketball	Diving	Gymnastics	Swimming	Track & Field	Triathlon
Barbara						
David						
Gerard						
Gina						
Sandra						
Tony						

Logic Puzzle 7

As part of the inaugural Nation Cup soccer tournament, five teams came from across America to play against each other. After all of the games were played, the event organizers tallied up the total number of goals that each team scored, as part of determining the tournament winner. In the end, the teams scored 2, 3, 4, 5, and 7 goals, in some order. From the clues below, can you determine what each team's nickname is, the city it's from (one was from Trenton), and how many goals it scored?

1. The Twins are not from a city that is a state capital.
2. The team from Pittsburgh scored more goals than the Blues.
3. The Orlando team scored 5 total goals.
4. Boise scored more goals than the Rangers, but fewer goals than the team that scored 4 goals.
5. The team from Boston and the Blues combined to score 10 goals.
6. The Giants scored an odd number of goals, but scored fewer goals than the Magic.

	Blues	Giants	Magic	Rangers	Twins	2	3	4	5	7
Boise										
Boston										
Orlando										
Pittsburgh										
Trenton										
2										
3										
4										
5										
7										

Logic Puzzle 8

At the newly opened Creature Café, monsters of all types were served some very *unique* foods. One day, five monsters came in to have lunch together. Each of them was a different type of monster, and each ordered a different item off the menu. Using the following clues, can you deduce what type of monster each was, and the item that each ordered?

1. Both Monica and the skeleton decided to pass on ordering the blood orange smoothie.
2. Wanda, the vampire, and the monster that ate the anchovy burger all went to the movies last week together to see the latest horror flick.
3. The five monsters, in no particular order, are Zack, the mummy, the one that ordered tarantula tortellini, Scarlet, and the one that ordered the fly soufflé.
4. The werewolf particularly enjoyed the snake salad.
5. Vlad was neither the mummy, nor did he order the fly soufflé.
6. Wanda loved the blood orange smoothie she ordered.
7. The skeleton and the monster that ordered the anchovy burger planned to meet up later for some green sludge tea and crumpets.
8. Scarlet was not a zombie.

	Anchovy Burger	Blood Orange Smoothie	Fly Soufflé	Snake Salad	Tarantula Tortellini	Mummy	Skeleton	Vampire	Werewolf	Zombie
Monica										
Scarlet										
Vlad										
Wanda										
Zack										
Mummy										
Skeleton										
Vampire										
Werewolf										
Zombie										

Math Road 1

A mathematical road is shown below. However, Thomas the Thief has stolen the mathematical operations from the road! Fill in each box with the appropriate operation (+ or -) so that you reach the target sum at the bottom of the road!

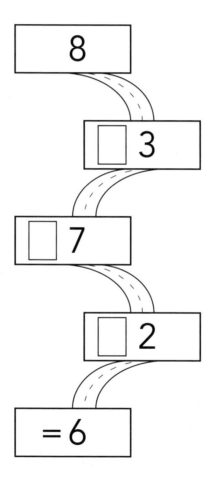

Math Road 2

A mathematical road is shown below. However, Thomas the Thief has stolen the mathematical operations from the road! Fill in each box with the appropriate operation (+ or -) so that you reach the target sum at the bottom of the road!

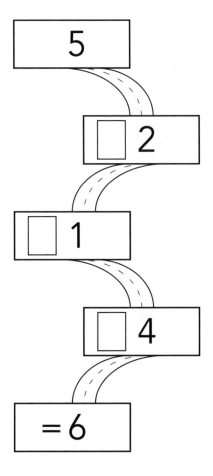

Math Road 3

A mathematical road is shown below. However, Thomas the Thief has stolen the mathematical operations from the road! Fill in each box with the appropriate operation (+ or -) so that you reach the target sum at the bottom of the road!

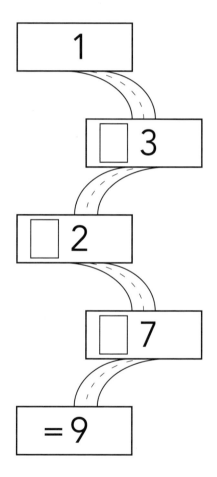

Math Road 4

A mathematical road is shown below. However, Thomas the Thief has stolen the mathematical operations from the road! Fill in each box with the appropriate operation (+ or -) so that you reach the target sum at the bottom of the road!

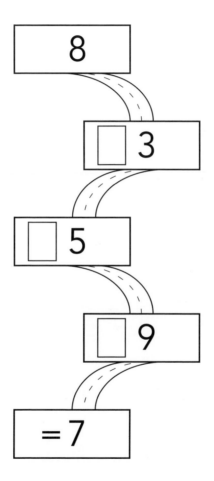

Math Road 5

A mathematical road is shown below. However, Thomas the Thief has stolen the mathematical operations from the road! Fill in each box with the appropriate operation (+ or -) so that you reach the target sum at the bottom of the road!

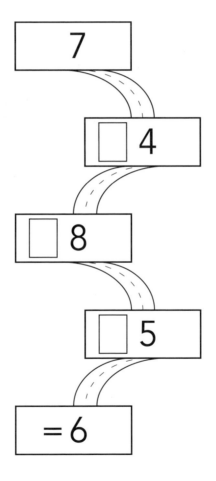

Math Road 6

A mathematical road is shown below. However, Thomas the Thief has stolen the mathematical operations from the road! Fill in each box with the appropriate operation (+ or -) so that you reach the target sum at the bottom of the road!

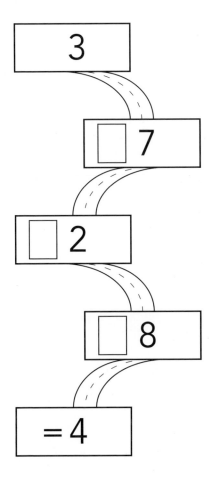

Math Road 7

A mathematical road is shown below. However, Thomas the Thief has stolen the mathematical operations from the road! Fill in each box with the appropriate operation (+ or -) so that you reach the target sum at the bottom of the road!

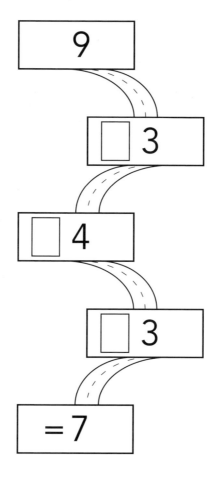

Math Road 8

A mathematical road is shown below. However, Thomas the Thief has stolen the mathematical operations from the road! Fill in each box with the appropriate operation (+ or -) so that you reach the target sum at the bottom of the road!

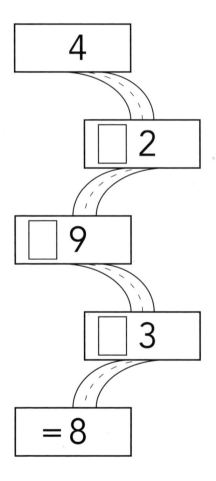

Math Road 9

A mathematical road is shown below. However, Thomas the Thief has stolen the mathematical operations from the road! Fill in each box with the appropriate operation (+, -, x, or ÷) so that you reach the target sum at the bottom of the road!

Note: Unlike previous math road puzzles, this is a little more tricky; you may need to use multiplication or division as well!

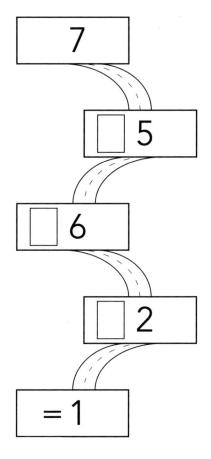

Math Road 10

A mathematical road is shown below. However, Thomas the Thief has stolen the mathematical operations from the road! Fill in each box with the appropriate operation (+, -, x, or ÷) so that you reach the target sum at the bottom of the road!

Note: Unlike previous math road puzzles, this is a little more tricky; you may need to use multiplication or division as well!

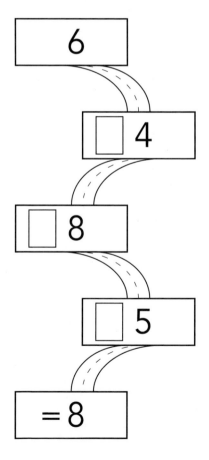

Maze 1

Help the cat find her way to her food bowl!

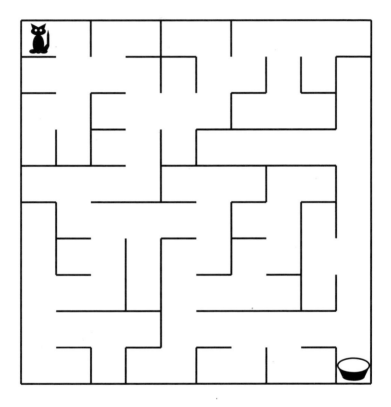

Maze 2

Help the cat find her way to her food bowl!

Maze 3

Help the cat find her way to her food bowl!

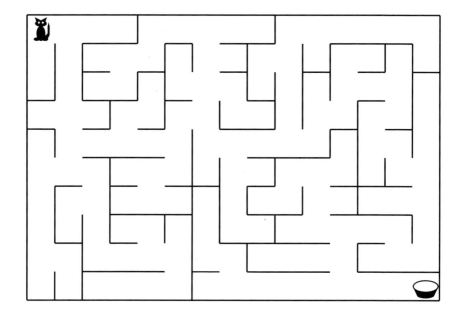

Maze 4

Help the cat find her way to her food bowl!

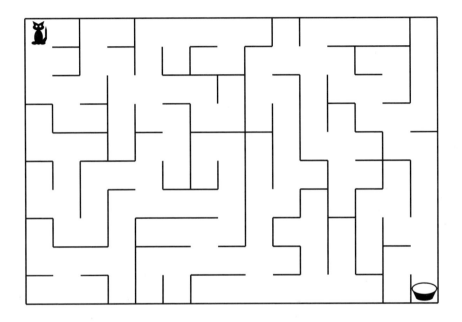

Maze 5

Help the cat find her way to her food bowl!

Maze 6

Help the cat find her way to her food bowl!

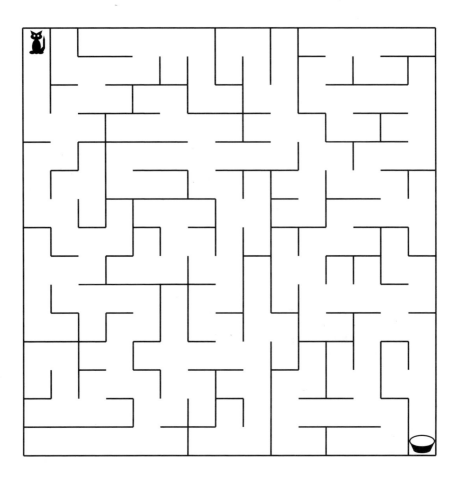

Maze 7

Help the cat find her way to her food bowl!

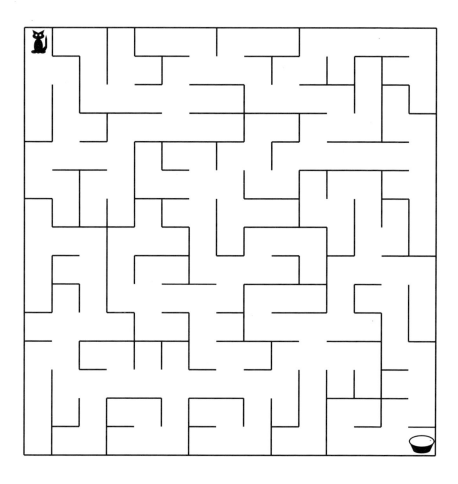

Maze 8

Help the cat find her way to her food bowl!

Maze 9

Help the cat find her way to her food bowl!

Maze 10

Help the cat find her way to her food bowl!

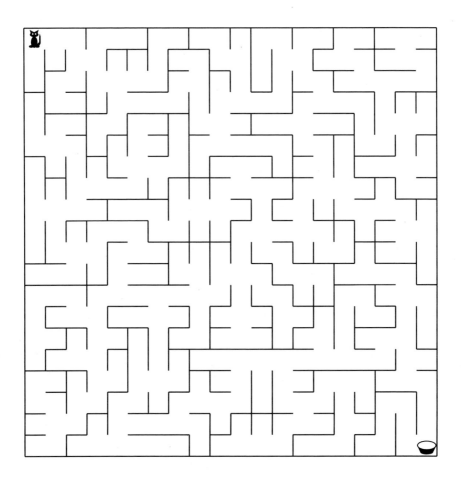

Hints

Word Clouds 1
The common theme is MLB team nicknames.

Word Clouds 2
The common theme is birds.

Word Clouds 3
The common theme is US presidents.

Word Clouds 4
The common theme is family members.

Word Clouds 5
The common theme is baby animals.

Word Clouds 6
The common theme is types of exercise.

Word Clouds 7
The common theme is fruit.

Encrypted Questions 1
Shift forward 1 letter (A→B, B→C, etc.).

Encrypted Questions 2
Shift forward 1 letter (A→B, B→C, etc.).

Encrypted Questions 3
Shift backward 1 letter (B→A, C→B, etc.).

Encrypted Questions 4
Shift backward 1 letter (B→A, C→B, etc.).

Encrypted Questions 5
Shift backward 1 letter (B→A, C→B, etc.).

Encrypted Questions 6
Shift forward 1 letter (A→B, B→C, etc.).

Encrypted Questions 7
Shift forward 1 letter (A→B, B→C, etc.).

Encrypted Questions 8
Shift backward 1 letter (B→A, C→B, etc.).

Encrypted Questions 9
Shift backward 2 letters (C→A, D→B, etc.).

Encrypted Questions 10
Shift forward 1 letter (A→B, B→C, etc.).

Encrypted Questions 11
Shift forward 2 letters (A→C, B→D, etc.).

Encrypted Questions 12
Shift forward 3 letters (A→D, B→E, etc.).

Encrypted Questions 13
Shift backward 4 letters (E→A, F→B, etc.).

Encrypted Questions 14
Shift forward 2 letters (A→C, B→D, etc.).

Encrypted Questions 15
Shift backward 1 letter (B→A, C→B, etc.).

Answer Keys

Sudoku 1

1	2	3	6	4	5
4	5	6	1	3	2
5	6	2	3	1	4
3	1	4	5	2	6
6	4	1	2	5	3
2	3	5	4	6	1

Sudoku 2

5	1	2	3	4	6
6	4	3	2	5	1
2	5	4	6	1	3
1	3	6	5	2	4
3	2	1	4	6	5
4	6	5	1	3	2

Sudoku 3

1	5	6	3	2	4
3	2	4	6	1	5
4	1	3	5	6	2
5	6	2	4	3	1
6	4	1	2	5	3
2	3	5	1	4	6

Sudoku 4

4	2	5	6	3	1
3	1	6	5	2	4
5	3	1	2	4	6
6	4	2	3	1	5
2	6	4	1	5	3
1	5	3	4	6	2

Sudoku 5

2	6	3	5	1	4
5	4	1	3	2	6
3	1	6	4	5	2
4	2	5	1	6	3
6	5	4	2	3	1
1	3	2	6	4	5

Sudoku 6

5	3	6	4	2	1
1	4	2	6	5	3
3	6	5	2	1	4
4	2	1	5	3	6
2	1	4	3	6	5
6	5	3	1	4	2

Sudoku 7

1	4	3	2	6	5
6	2	5	4	1	3
4	3	2	6	5	1
5	6	1	3	4	2
3	1	4	5	2	6
2	5	6	1	3	4

Sudoku 8

1	3	2	6	5	4
6	4	5	3	1	2
3	2	4	5	6	1
5	6	1	2	4	3
4	5	3	1	2	6
2	1	6	4	3	5

Sudoku 9

7	6	2	4	5	8	3	1
5	8	3	1	7	6	4	2
3	2	6	8	1	4	7	5
1	4	7	5	3	2	6	8
8	7	5	3	6	1	2	4
2	1	4	6	8	7	5	3
4	5	1	7	2	3	8	6
6	3	8	2	4	5	1	7

Sudoku 10

1	7	5	8	4	3	6	2
3	2	4	6	1	7	8	5
2	6	3	4	7	1	5	8
7	4	6	5	2	8	1	3
8	3	1	2	6	5	4	7
5	1	8	7	3	4	2	6
6	5	7	1	8	2	3	4
4	8	2	3	5	6	7	1

Word Search 1

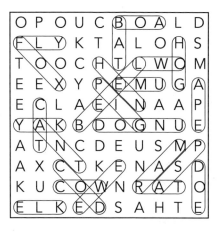

Word Search 2

Word Search 3

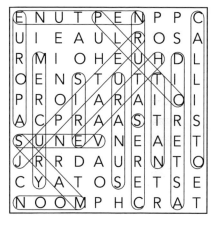

Word Search 4

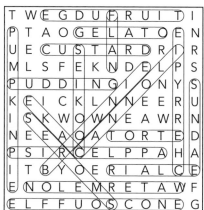

Word Search 5

Word Search 6

Word Search 7

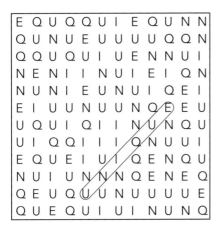

Word Search 8

Word Search 9

```
E  D  N  D  D  L  E  E  D  N  E  E
D  L  E  L  E  E  L  L  N  N  D  D
E  D  D  L  D  L  L  E  N  E  E  E
N  E  E  E  E  D  E  E  N  E  E
E  D  E  E  N  E  E  E  E  L  E  N
E  D  E  E  E  N  N  E  E  L  N
E  D  E  N  L  D  L  E  D  N  E  E
E  E  D  N  N  E  D  D  E  E  E  E
L  N  E  E  D  N  E  E  N  D  E  E
D  N  E  L  E  L  E  E  D  E  E  E
D  D  E  N  D  L  E  N  L  L  N  E
D  L  E  D  N  E  L  E  E  N  E  D
```

Word Clouds 1

The common theme is MLB team nicknames. The words are: RED SOX, YANKEES, ORIOLES, GIANTS, CARDINALS, TWINS, BREWERS, PIRATES, METS.

Word Clouds 2

The common theme is birds. The words are: EAGLE, VULTURE, GOOSE, SEAGULL, HUMMINGBIRD, HAWK, OSTRICH, PIGEON, PEACOCK.

Word Clouds 3

The common theme is US presidents. The words are: WASHINGTON, ADAMS, LINCOLN, ROOSEVELT, HARRISON, TAFT, CARTER, REAGAN, CLINTON.

Word Clouds 4

The common theme is family members. The words are: MOTHER, FATHER, SISTER, BROTHER, UNCLE, AUNT, GRANDMA, NIECE, NEPHEW.

Word Clouds 5

The common theme is baby animals. The words are: CALF, JOEY, PIGLET, TADPOLE, CHICK, FAWN, KITTEN, DUCKLING, FOAL.

Word Clouds 6

The common theme is types of exercise. The words are: SWIMMING, BIKING, RUNNING, DANCING, WALKING, CLIMBING, SWINGING, DIVING, HURDLING.

Word Clouds 7

The common theme is fruit. The words are: APPLE, PEACH, STRAWBERRY, BLUEBERRY, KIWI, RASPBERRY, PINEAPPLE, ORANGE, GRAPE.

Hidden Words 1
Cat, Otter, Owl

Hidden Words 2
Eel, Horse, Asp

Hidden Words 3
Spain, Iran, China

Hidden Words 4
India, Peru, Iceland

Hidden Words 5
Oregon, Maine, Colorado

Hidden Words 6
Idaho, Alaska, Utah

Hidden Words 7
Train, Plane, Car

Hidden Words 8
Truck, Boat, Van

Hidden Words 9
Tea, Water, Soda

Hidden Words 10
Apple, Ham, Bean

Hidden Words 11
Dragon, Fairy, Elf

Encrypted Questions 1

WHY DID THE SKELETON DECIDE NOT TO GO TO THE DANCE?

IT HAD NO BODY TO DANCE WITH.

Encrypted Questions 2

DID YOU HEAR THE JOKE ABOUT THE THREE HOLES IN THE GROUND?

WELL . . . WELL . . . WELL . . .

Encrypted Questions 3

DID YOU HEAR THE JOKE ABOUT THE JUMP ROPE?

IT'S TOO LONG. LET'S JUST SKIP IT.

Encrypted Questions 4

WHY DO PEOPLE HEAR MUSIC PLAYING BACKWARDS AT BEETHOVEN'S GRAVE?

HE IS DECOMPOSING.

Encrypted Questions 5

WHAT DID THE DIVERS FIND SHAKING AT THE BOTTOM OF THE OCEAN?

A NERVOUS WRECK

Encrypted Questions 6

WHY WAS THE FARMER'S SON SHAKING THE COWS?

HE WANTED A MILKSHAKE.

Encrypted Questions 7

HOW DID THE COOKIE FEEL WHEN IT WOKE UP?

CHIP-PER

Encrypted Questions 8

WHY COULDN'T THE PIRATE RECITE THE ALPHABET?

HE ALWAYS GOT LOST AT C.

Encrypted Questions 9

WHAT SOUND DOES A SLEEPING TRICERATOPS MAKE?

A DINO-SNORE

Encrypted Questions 10

WHAT DID THE CLOUD WEAR UNDER ITS SHORTS?

THUNDERWEAR

Encrypted Questions 11

WHAT DID THE OCEAN SAY TO THE BEACH?

NOTHING. IT JUST WAVED.

Encrypted Questions 12

WHAT IS A CAT'S FAVORITE COLOR?

PURR-PLE

Encrypted Questions 13

WHERE DO YOU LEARN HOW TO MAKE A BANANA SPLIT?

SUNDAE SCHOOL

Encrypted Questions 14

I ASKED MY DOG IF SHE COULD TELL ME WHAT FOUR MINUS FOUR IS.

SHE SAID NOTHING.

Encrypted Questions 15

MY DAD SAID THE MATH JOKES HE TELLS ME AREN'T ALL BAD.

JUST SUM ARE.

Pyramid 1

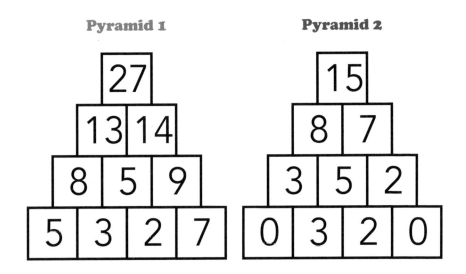

Pyramid 2

Pyramid 3

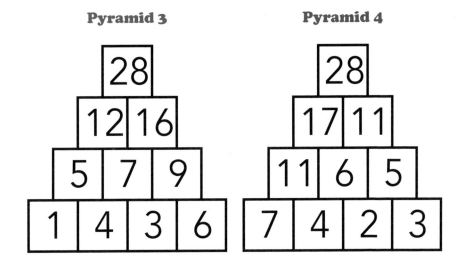

Pyramid 4

Pyramid 5

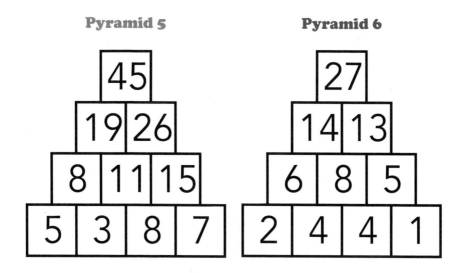

Pyramid 6

Pyramid 7

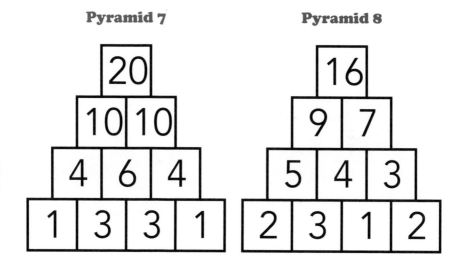

Pyramid 8

Pyramid 9

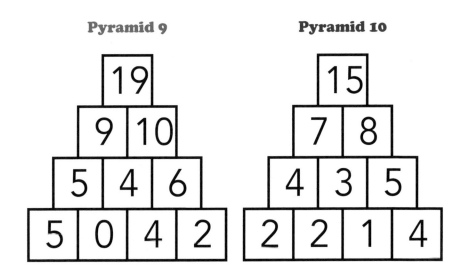

	19		
9	10		
5	4	6	
5	0	4	2

Pyramid 10

	15		
7	8		
4	3	5	
2	2	1	4

Spot the Same 1
A and F

Spot the Same 2
C and E

Spot the Same 3
A and E

Spot the Same 4
A and F

Spot the Same 5
B and H

Spot the Same 6
B and G

Spot the Same 7
A and F

Spot the Same 8
D and I

Spot the Same 9
F and G

Spot the Same 10
E and H

Logic Puzzle 1

Barbara had the blue dragon.
Charlie had the white dragon.
Molly had the green dragon.
Robert had the red dragon.
Susan had the black dragon.

Logic Puzzle 2

Elizabeth was 1st.
Al was 2nd.
David was 3rd.
Billy was 4th.
Connie was 5th.

Logic Puzzle 3

Marian liked the whale.
Nora liked the manatee.
Polly liked the shark.
Robert liked the flounder.
Sebastian liked the crab.

Logic Puzzle 4

Buddy likes history.
Cindy likes chemistry.
Deb likes physical education.
Evan likes English.
Frank likes geometry.
Gail likes French.

Logic Puzzle 5

Annie liked the cow at 9:30 a.m.
Brenda liked the giraffe at 10:30 a.m.
Caroline liked the pig at 11:00 a.m.
Dawn liked the rooster at 9:00 a.m.
Ezekiel liked the horse at 10:00 a.m.

Logic Puzzle 6

Barbara trained for the triathlon.
David trained for track & field.
Gerard trained for diving.
Gina trained for swimming.
Sandra trained for basketball.
Tony trained for gymnastics.

Logic Puzzle 7

Boise Blues scored 3 goals.
Boston Magic scored 7 goals.
Orlando Giants scored 5 goals.
Pittsburgh Twins scored 4 goals.
Trenton Rangers scored 2 goals.

Logic Puzzle 8

Monica the vampire likes the Fly
   Souffle.
Scarlet the werewolf likes the
   Snake Salad.
Vlad the skeleton likes the
   Tarantula Tortellini.
Wanda the mummy likes the Blood
   Orange Smoothie.
Zack the zombie likes the Anchovy
   Burger.

Math Road 1
8+3-7+2=6

Math Road 2
5-2-1+4=6

Math Road 3
1+3-2+7=9

Math Road 4
8+3+5-9=7

Math Road 5
7-4+8-5=6

Math Road 6
3+7+2-8=4

Math Road 7
9-3+4-3=7

Math Road 8
4-2+9-3=8

Math Road 9
(7+5) ÷6 ÷2=1

Math Road 10
6x4÷8+5=8

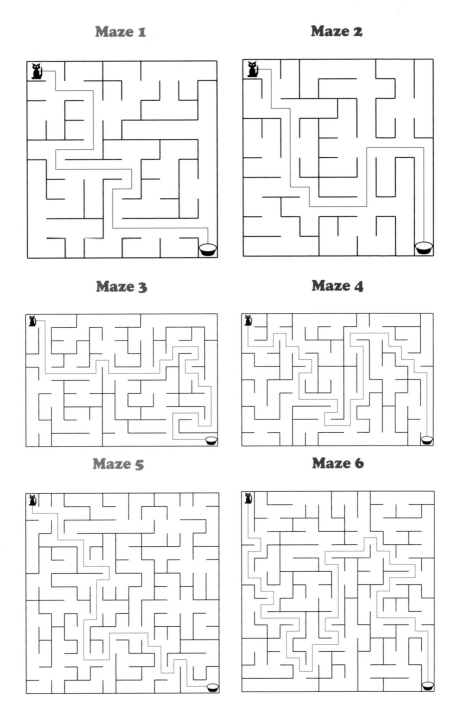

Maze 1

Maze 2

Maze 3

Maze 4

Maze 5

Maze 6